ALL SAINTS

BRENDA MARIE OSBEY

ALL SAINTS

New

and

Selected

Poems

LOUISIANA STATE UNIVERSITY PRESS

Baton Rouge

1997

08 07 06 05 04 03 02 01 00 99   6 5 4 3 2

Designer: Amanda McDonald Key
Typeface Display Optima, text Bembo

Library of Congress Cataloging-in-Publication Data

Osbey, Brenda Marie.
  All saints : new and selected poems / Brenda Marie Osbey.
    p. cm.
  ISBN 0-8071-2197-5 (cloth alk paper) —ISBN 0-8071-2198-3
  (pbk . alk paper)
  I. Title.
  PS3565 S33A79 1997
  811'.54—dc21   97-19936
                                                            CIP

The paper in this book meets the guidelines for permanence and durability of the Committee on Production Guidelines for Book Longevity of the Council on Library Resources. ∞

The author gratefully acknowledges the editors of the following publications, in which some of these poems first appeared: *American Poetry Review* ("Elvena", "Everything Happens to [Monk and] Me", "Expeditus"; "The Head of Luís Congo Congo Speaks"; "House of the Dead Remembering [House of Mercies/Variation 2]", "Speaking of Trains"), *American Voice* ("The Business of Pursuit San Malo's Prayer", "The Evening News: A Letter to Nina Simone", "Stones of Soweto"), *Callaloo* ("Desire and Private Griefs"), *Indiana Review* ("Sor Juana"), *Southern Review* ("Another Time and Farther South" ; "Mother Catherine"), and *2 PLUS2. A Collection of International Writing* ("Alberta [Factory Poem/Variation 2]", "Peculiar Fascination with the Dead", "Faubourg Study No. 3: The Seven Sisters on New Orleans").

The author also wishes to thank Andrew Antippas and Barrister's Gallery of New Orleans

To the memory of

Louis Allen Hamilton, Jr.

and

Alberta Vivian Cobb Hamilton

CONTENTS

1. LIVE AMONG YOUR DEAD, WHOM YOU HAVE EVERY RIGHT TO LOVE

For Charles H. Rowell, On the Death of His Father / 3

Desire and Private Griefs / 6

Stones of Soweto / 11

Alberta (Factory Poem/Variation 2) / 15

Another Time and Farther South / 20

House of the Dead Remembering (House of Mercies/
      Variation 2) / 22

Peculiar Fascination with the Dead / 25

2. IN THE FAUBOURG

Faubourg / 37

Faubourg Study No. 3: The Seven Sisters of New
      Orleans / 39

The Evening News: A Letter to Nina Simone / 54

Speaking of Trains / 63

Elvena / 70

Everything Happens to (Monk and) Me / 74

3. EX VOTOS

Mother Catherine / 81

St. Martin / 85

Sor Juana / 88

The Head of Luís Congo Speaks / 98

Expeditus / 104

The Business of Pursuit: San Malo's Prayer / 108

Suicide City / 115

Glossary of New Orleans Ethnic Expressions, Place Names, and Characters / 123

Biography / 128

INVOCATION

The slave ancestors who lie beneath the swamps, inside the
brick of which our
homes, our streets, our churches are made;
who wrought iron into the vèvès that hold together the Old
City and its attachments;
personal gods and ancestors; musicians and street dancers;
Hoodoo saints and their little Catholic cousins . . .
our saints continue to live among us.

> *May they never leave us.*
> *May the newly sanctified find their way home to us also.*
> *May they feed well and be pleased with these offerings.*
> *And soon*
> *One day*
> *May we all be counted among them.*

1.

live among your dead,

whom you have every right

to love

For Charles H. Rowell, On the Death of His Father

1.

go tell them i have laid down my yard shoes
my house keys, my dead wife's handkerchief box
and the sight of my children
leaning at my face
in old photographs on the livingroom walls
and their voices saying
it was then
i saw it
he was with me in the field
we saw the brown dust when it covered the evening
all of these things:
i have laid them all by.

they are mourning me
and i am still a living man.

2.

my father stood in the field that evening
sifting the brown earth
through his turned–up fingers.
walking a little behind him
i was going through words in my head
testing how they sounded
in the empty expanse of the land.
he said something about a nephew
nathan or somebody.
i pulled on my cigarette
and watched him stretch his arm
across my line of vision
motioning over the field.

3.

my mouth is a barren plot of ground
a sand–colored silence
where my children stand hollow
over breakfast
two rooms away.
they discuss their mother
and the color of my urine.
they make these little sounds
eruptions i am not yet used to.
my death is in their throats and lungs.
they swallow hard before entering my bedroom.
my used body parts
are already in the grave.
i wonder can they see
how my soul is a grey fog
creeping the fertile land outside this window
to the left of the house?
but they want me to say something
because all my life
my name has been josiah.

4.

it is over now.
people are calling me long–distance.
writing on postcards
telling me how best to grieve.
they do not know that the young do not mourn.
they do not know that my hands are empty buckets
easily weighted to the ground with such stones.
they see me move both feet in succession
and rub my back with funeral lore.
etherine sings about *sweet peace.*
the others say *yes*
and talk of *going on.*

but then,
they have never seen the brown dustclouds
rolling over the rich alabama soil *red*
on my daddy's land.

Desire and Private Griefs

1.

the kind of man you would call on
to carry your dead mother up on his shoulders
a genuine furrow lining his brow
settling down her remains
with the grace of one who had expected to be called
at just such a time
and so had come prepared to do his duty
by the living
the dead
had not turned his back on your grieving
but stood somewhat apart
some respectful distance
between the sight of your huge grief
and the guilty love you had come to put to rest.

i named him that first time
—sterling, son—
some dead uncle's name.
even then i could see he knew
the turning away that comes to even the bravest.
and then there was the challenge of this hunger
writing the years
across my body.

it was a dangerous affair from the start.

2.

the first thing you learn about desire
is that it does not wear down with time.
there comes a time
when you can no longer get your pleasure
but the desire stays with you—

a dampish kind of feeling
beneath the armpits
at the back of the tongue.

i stand across a banquet hall from him
a desk
a room
the gravesite of someone i cared too little for in life.
he will not look into my face.
(the damp.
the quiet.)
i take him home
accustomed to the kinds of rumors generated
at times like this.
(he has the weary look he wears so beautifully
and tracks graveyard dust
onto my freshly cleaned floors.)
i do not touch him until he is naked
his head cradled lightly
in the damp bend of my lap.

it is all so familiar—
the cleaving
the hunger
the years do not relieve.
years pass.
one day no reply will come at all.
(an aunt or someone who knew us both
will send the news.
it will do no good trying to get home in time.
they will have laid him aside
weeks before i can have known.
a newspaper clipping
a photograph from years ago.)
how can it have gone on so long?
he means his own longevity
my returning ever so often only to find

ruined cities i must go to immediately
the meetings on the floors of jazz clubs and cultural cau
    cus affairs
the grey hairs heaped upon his head
his heart greying against me
the inability to give or get satisfaction
in spite of all the rubbing in the dark.
he will not ask for mercy
and i make no offers, no kind gestures.

it was a dangerous affair from the beginning he says to me.
he looks at me across a tiny, papered table.
i do not hear the claims he makes.
i know better.
and i do not pretend to be a kind woman.

later
he goes with me to the airport.
i'm too old for this his smile wants to say.
been too old for this a long time now.
the first thing you learn about desire i almost answer,
it will eat you alive. if you let it.
he puts a cigarette to his mouth as if to ask *how long?*
i step out from the checker cab
—years pass—
i too begin to bury my dead
begin to grey along the edges.
nothing ends.

3.

cairo
madrid
aix-les-bains
brazil
antigua
i send him cards

letters.
wherever i go
i sit down to write.
sometimes he replies
not often
but well.
we understand one another
—finally—
and it has taken so long.

he sends photographs
his head gone completely white
a brief smile.
his letters do not mention
the names of the dead he continues to bury—
relatives
friends
the relatives of childhood playmates.
he talks to me of aging.
if i were younger one letter begins.
my own letters
often are no more than travelogues
landscapes at best.
his maps of time—
bottled and stoppered
—though less than airtight—
and carry the motley smells
of home.

i send him gifts—
my fingernails
twists of hair from the nape of my neck
scarves i find in trinidad and algiers.

4.

death changes some things:

the way you feel about your mother
the path you take to get to a cousin's house
the greetings you give out
at casual meetings and such
the kind of woman you call on
to stand for your dead
—a genuine sorrow drawn across her face—
you trust her to grieve for you
without interfering in your fate.

she will not speak of guilts and broken promises
the losses she has suffered
written plainly beneath her eyes.
she lends an air of grace to the procession
the only woman not wearing black—
a tan or charcoal grey dress
altogether lacking in severity
hat cocked to one side
feathers and jewels—
she looks across the gravesite
a certain blankness to her stare.
she turns only after the others have done so—
a private grief that does not surface.

she leaves alone
carrying the heavy silences
of the dead.

Stones of Soweto

A Mourning Poem for Moses Nkondo

our recent dead have no shame.
they stand among the daily stuff of our lives
insisting on remembrance
attending the first signs
of forgetfulness or sloth
to damn us with their silence
the violent quiet the dead know
as no others do—
the holes they have left
in what we call our lives.

no. i do not forget.
part of me goes dutifully into the ground
where my father's own dust
makes its place among the hard
and equally silent stones,
down where you wait
for the heady remembrance
of other sons like me
who have yet to die.
how will you know me
—any of us—
from all of the others
calling out to their dead
among the clamoring stones and dust of soweto?

no, mother.
no.
now that you are also gone
now i can speak my small withered truth.
i do not believe in religions
no matter how well grounded
in the truths of our marrow
nor in final rest
—only the silence that enshrouds us

and gives no relief when i call out "mother."
only memory
—that is something like prayer.
and how will you tell me
from among all the other mourners
calling out to their dead
among the stones of this city?
how will i know you are not turning
ever turning to the cries
equally resonant
equally late
of other sons
of sons not yours
also folding dark arms upon dark hearts
oceans and oceans
away from home?

i sit and talk.
i sit and write.
i walk or drive the streets of new england and new york.
and all around me
death walks like a loose woman along these city streets.
down south friends tell me
the catalpa trees
bear heavy mottled flowers
out of season
and in the rain.
i am only one man
full of my own little words
and perhaps no great gift as a son.
it is true i am silent.
it is true i do not weep
or shout
or pray
or curse the lonely fates.
but i am only one man
lifetimes away

from all i have called home.
and my grief when it comes
is like a train whistle in the night—
if you sleep soundly
you will never know how it came or went
or how many souls it left standing
empty-handed along its tracks.
and anyway
the night is dark like me
and so soon gone.

i tell you mother
i stand worlds and worlds away from your rest.
i did not see your face in death
but your living face
i have carried in my deepest places all these years.
i can even say
that once i saw you cry.
i walked into your and my father's bedroom
only to find you sitting there
pools of tears
in your two cupped palms.
perhaps no.
perhaps it was not like that.
nothing like that at all.
but that was many years ago.
i was a boy.
and i had never seen you weep before.
nor does it matter why you wept.
you wept your tears.
i saw them.
i must have stood
—a mute fool—
some time before i looked away.
but that was many years ago.
i was a boy.
perhaps you yourself will not even recall.

but your living face, mother
i carry in my deepest places.

i stand on some anonymous bridge
above some body
of cold and moving water.
i do not smoke cigarettes or carry change
and so have nothing
to toss in.
from where i stand i see no reflection
save some vast and murky sky.
it could be any time of year.
i am not cold.
i stand and look across the water.
it could be any time of year.
i could be any man.
i am your son nonetheless.
i know your name.
i carry your face in my deepest places.
i do not believe in gods and their musings.
i do not believe
only in silence
and memory
that is something like prayer.
i believe in my own name
and the many clamoring stones
of soweto.

Alberta *(Factory Poem/Variation 2)*

1.

when my grandmother alberta was a girl
she worked in solomon's factory
alongside
women
who stood to stitch men's suits
to hang from the shoulders of white mannequins
who would not say *thank you*
for the any number of needles sewn through flesh
to put food on the table
to keep children in school
or a husband home
to avoid the indignity of government "relief"
to protect a mother or a father
from the old folks' home.

my grandmother alberta was a girl when she first saw
women eating small sandwiches
or bread dry-long-so
from the hip-pockets of their dresses
as they stood sewing
because they were given no time for lunch.
women bleeding through triple-layered toweling
afraid to leave their machines the length of time it took
to wash and change the wadded cloth between their legs
afraid to lose the pay
solomon's sons doled out at week's end.
and more than once
a woman who had to go—
but not soon enough.
a woman sprawled against the white commode
the dark fluid slipping across the floor
and the two or three other women
standing guard against the door

hiding away the solution:
quinine and castor oil
to bring on the quick violent abortion
that might let you stagger back to a machine
to stand and stitch together
collars and lapels
welt pockets to decorate white mannequins
propped up in better stores
throughout the southern region.

she was a woman with a husband and children
by the time she knelt
between her own baby sister's knees
and caught the nearly full-term moving mass
felt its warm head in her hand
before she flushed it down the toilet
and wiped between galena's legs.
all kinds of things i saw and did she said
working in a factory of women

and it was no time
before she was promoted to floor-walker
freed from the stooping posture
of those women who stitched
heads down in silence
or singing across to one another
lyrics spun out above the hum of motors and needles.
often it was the threadcutters
whose bottoms bore into the long wooden benches
where they squatted gap-kneed more than sat
who tossed out a line
and it would come back
stretched by the heavier voice
of some woman who stood all day
wiping the oil from her fingers
into the blackened wood
of her upright atlas machine.

such a woman sent back a line stretched to endurance
altogether seamless
against the drone of motors
working at full pitch.
my grandmother alberta walked the boarded spaces between
       the women.
she walked.
she kept time.
is it any wonder she asks
as if i were to answer
is it any wonder
we sang like that?

2.

a great deal happened the year i was nine.
so i suppose i must have been nine the year my mother
not my grandmother
taught me to embroider.
i sat cross-legged on the hard floor
bunching upon the coarse cloth
that would become
dishcloths
tea cozies
for my grandmother
who surely had enough of one
and small use for the other.
later
much later
i learned to fashion
elaborately flowered pillowslips
dresser scarves
lace edgings she loved to store up
to show off to relatives
foolish enough to visit
during the long new orleans summers.

your mother does a fine stitch she says
watching me lift then re-set
the heavy iron over the face-down designs
as i was taught.
when i do not look up from my task
she offers at a lower register:
sewing is different
no one teaches you to sew.

3.

the men who worked the mezzanine
the cutting floor above
looked out across the vast crowded floor of women,
rolled up white shirtsleeves,
took white chalk in hand,
marking and cutting.
men's labor.
calling for a certain daring precision.
and higher paying
affording short breaks
to smoke or eat
to drink rc cola on the stair landing
to take time to look across the crowded floor of women
on the ground level
manufacturing blues.

4.

"we stood together.
we worked together.
we cussed old man solomon
and the day he ever set foot inside this city.
we cursed the cloth we stitched together
and the lives it cost us to stitch it.
we cursed the babies we dropped

18

and the men who gave them to us,
the bodies, our own bodies,
that held to them in the womb,
the conditions that dogged us so
and made us drop them
by choice or by accident
by long standing in heat or cold,
the perfect solution handed over to us
by the women we stood among,
manufacturing blues
for all we were worth."

these are the last words
the words my grandmother alberta
did not say to me.
my grandmother alberta is dead.
she cannot speak to me further
of her youth among those women
her and her baby sister
down on the ground level
among their upright atlas machines.
she can no longer hold up at eye level
her slightly yellowed middle finger
sewn through the nail
the smooth even split
where the machine tore flesh and nail
and after all those years
the nail refused ever to grow together.
my grandmother alberta is dead and buried
and reduced to ash.
i am her last remaining evidence:
the smooth
straight
seam.

Another Time and Farther South

for Clyde R. Taylor, A Mourning Poem

in another time and farther south
i would give you ashes for your dead
clean white kerchieves of linen or hand-worked silk
spread crushed shell before you
and tell you to kneel there
and weep in dignity
like a man.
but these are times of strangeness; we are no kin.
and this cold dry air of your native northeast
can not tend such an aesthetic
as these gifts of mourning would require.
so who am i to tell a man i barely know or love
to kneel in the dust of pride and much remembering
weeping loudly for the death of a mother
that no memory of pain can take away
and no amount of sorrow can return?
can i say death is one more burden, friend
and we bear it with us into even this driest earth?
can i tell you there is no time passing
no fondness in the eyes of friends that will return to you
the life of the only woman to warm you in her belly
and give to you the very life and air you live and breathe
the blood that warms you
so much of what you think you know and have forgotten?
no.
these are words and stand for nothing more.
but i can say that in another time and so much farther south
i could have led you through the streets in ashes
one of several women bearing you along
to some sainted spirit-ground you could believe on—
a man who had lost his mother, still a son.
and we, the cluster of women
could stand aside beneath the palms
pressing roots of ginger underfoot.

watching you learn the lesson only death would ever teach:

how you can lose so much in life
and walk upon the earth a living man
wearing all the shrouds of mourning like a skin
and memory like a stone inside your organs
alone for all the rituals of yielding, giving up
and still walk home
finding your way among strewn ashes in the dark.

House of the Dead Remembering
(House of Mercies/Variation 2)

this bone-sack you see
held together with twine worn almost smooth
once danced and shook the bamboula.
now it makes one piece
with the blues you bring me
served up like sunday dinner
the borrowed sound
of your borrowed hurt
neatly arranged by the same brown fingers
that touch my face
and tend the plants out back.
and the days like an old man in soft-soled shoes
picking up his walk
from the backs of his thighs
remembering to catch up his pants knees
before squatting to sit
in the company of women.

this chamy bag holds together the past
of the house where i was born
house of mercies
made of dry rot and tenpenny nails
house of mercies
holding up the sky
keeping it from falling
into the swampy earth
house of mercies
where my mother ate the dry bread of silence
where my grandfather managed
to stride through death unaided
upright
through the front-room window
of the house he built
where my grandmother insisted
that as children we learn

the many proper ways
to honor our dead
because memory is everything.

and what is it you bring me
carried in your arms
like a stillborn child you insist on naming?
nothing more than your own bruised past
rolled between the fingers of your good left hand
and treated like trouble
because you want more from me
than this fallow language
would have you say.
why can't you see
how we are both just borrowed against time
like so much grieving
saved up in the corners of a house
that recognizes no past
and everyone goes on living
only to honor the dead
to eat this dry crust
without relish
or desire?

your youth is gone.
my youth is leaving me.
you want what i want:
some guarantee against forgetfulness
in the way we go about our lives
some proof that death is something more
than throwing dirt in the face
and turning to walk away
some hope against the awesome forgetting
when we go into the ground.

when we were younger
and i moved against you in the bed mama left me
your eyes part closed

your mouth open
breathing loud
do you remember what you used to say?
loose me, loose me
i held you even closer
dragging you quicker and deeper
into the smell of our locked bodies
my bones
your bones
my body that carried no children to remember us by
loose me you begged me
but i never set you free.
memory is everything.

you sit in the room
you outfitted for yourself.
i sit at my desk
facing out on the slave-bricked street below.
we want to believe
in the both of our lives
of passion and much grieving.
we want some proper antidote
to the pasts we have accumulated
living as we have
in this house of death and remembering
the dry crusts of our younger selves
like so many photographs
scattered among the objects
that measure out our years

the architecture of two lovers
growing old
in a wood-framed house
and nothing more.

Peculiar Fascination with the Dead

light candles to honor the dead.
set flowers on the altars of the dead
which must be raised in your home.
wear the memory of the dead plainly
so anyone looking will see
how the decent do not forget.
speak of the dead
as though you thought they might hear
from the adjoining room.
keep mourning portraits
always about your home.
marry memory to the dead.
put silver coins in the corners of your rooms.
pray for the dead.
go into the tombed cities
along basin, canal boulevard, valence and esplanade;
carry flowering plants
bits of brown paper
smooth stones
the burdens of what time you have left
to honor the dead
as they ought to be honored.
live among your dead,
whom you have every right
to love.

part one:
it is 1969.
i go alone with my brother for the first time
to our grandfather's grave.
we search among the tangled growth.
my brother finds a skull.
i refuse to touch it.
he sees i am afraid.
it's dead, he smiles.

it can't hurt you.
i don't like the way he says *it.*
surely death
is more complex than that.
but i am twelve
and a girl besides.
twenty
thirty minutes
maybe more.
we find papa's headboard.
when the gravetender turns his back
my brother puts the skull
into the brown paper sack that carries our tools.
i look at him a long while.
he does not care.
he bends down
and begins weeding.

later
at home
when he pulls out his skull during dessert
our grandmother slumps into her coffee.
it's not papa's head, he offers in self-defense.
mama stops tending her mother
to slap one side of his head:
get up from this table
and take that thing from this house, now.
i sweat.
my face turns cold.
catch your sister, i hear mama order him
before she hits the floor.

some days later
i find the skull beneath the front porch steps.
i tell mama.
she looks at me in disbelief.
following me to the spot.

when he comes home
she takes him by the shoulders:
you are taking that thing back where it belongs
back where you found it.
say nothing.
tomorrow morning we take the bus to the cemetery.
don't you answer me back, child.
my patience with you
is wearing thin.

i did not take the bus ride that next morning.
who wants to see her mother
walking about
among the tumbledown graves no one cares for
and the gravetender in his overalls
pretending not to see
looking at your slender mother
in her straight gabardine skirt
pitchblack hair swinging down her back
sweat breaking out on her forehead
above her lip
even though everyone knows
it is always cool inside the cemetery gates?
who wants to see her mother
stop before her own father's grave.
the favorite daughter
admiring the work of two children
learning to honor the dead?
i stayed home with my grandmother.

we play bingo.
she lets me win twice.
we eat black-eyed peas.
she looks at the clock a lot.
she makes us both hot toddies
and makes me promise not to tell.
i worm up close to her:

the smell of tweed
and sugared whiskey.
we climb into her double bed
even though it is still early.
we nap until they wake us.
mama has brownies.
we agree to save them for the late night movies
she says we can all stay up for.
mama sits on her bed
wearing only the blue slip
with the pleated bottom.
her skin is like new pennies.
she puts her hand to her forehead that way.
she lets me watch her
without snapping her eyes the way she sometimes does
if i stare too long.
i remember how she looked
after being in the graves all morning.

i was twelve years old.
it was 1969.

part two:
let the dead rest.
please.
she was our sister.
why must you always talk such dirt?
she was the one told you
about that damned husband of yours
but you had to hear it on the streets.
even so, you kept him.
she was your sister.
you will not speak of her that way.
not in my house
not in the house my dead husband built me
with his own two hands.

my grandmother alberta's younger sister
has a hump in her back.
it comes, they say
from all those years in the factory:
her slight body
bent over the sewing machines
standing the long hours into evening
trying to keep one eye on her husband
working on the mezzanine above:
the cutting floor
where the men earned so much more money
whisking out collars and lapels
from fabric and stiffening,
and the few girl-women who ran their errands
fetching new blades on command
trying to avoid
the swift dry hands
that ran up their dresses.
at least the decent ones tried.

part three:
the mourning portrait.
uncle son in his casket
dressed to kill.
features pulled tight across his skull
death mask of a self
that danced and cried
ate red beans and rice
made love to women
refused to marry
until he fell ill.
they never knew what killed him
a heart weakened by strong drink, rich food,
or lorraine's deep grudge:
some fix choking the life from him
as he lay half asleep in her bed.
if not her

then any one of the others.
we never will know what it was.

my grandmother kept the portrait.
the other sisters would not have it.
their younger brother
dressed in his best suit
—of which there were dozens—
some perfect white shirt,
almost his most handsome self:
the clear brown skin
with its waxy glow of death,
the grey silk pillow beneath his head
his greying hair cut close
brushed back,
the perfectly manicured hands.
they say they don't bury you
with shoes on your feet.
my grandmother said she had no idea.
she knew they buried him with his rings.
the gold watch and chain some woman had given him
did not go into the grave—
not from respect for his two widows,
but what need has a dead man
for the passing of measured time?

part four:
the people sit about like shadows of other people
lined about the walls
of the room we all have gathered in
to wake ms. munday.
i want to know how she will get up

> *the first three nights in the grave are the saddest.*
> *only then do the dead know*
> *they have left behind their families.*

and there is no comfort
to bury such loss.
we sit with our dead the first night
to show we are not afraid to go on
and then we set them free.
we must not burden our dead.
those first three nights are carriage enough.
and we want to be well-remembered
even among the graves
the walled cities
of the dead.

if she's still dead.
my grandmother does not answer.
be quiet child, she says to me.
the dead go into the ground.

we waked ms. munday until midnight.
she did not rise up.
not even for rev. munday sitting at the foot of her casket
looking toward the back room
of what had been their home.
i thought she and death were the same thing.
even in life she had not been so pale,
that tarnished white.
like bones a dog plays with in the neighbor's side-alley
but will not eat.
that is why white is a mourning color:
the spirit takes off
leaving no sign
of substance or color.

there is not much else i remember.
i fell asleep
across my grandmother alberta's thighs—
the smell of mavis talcum
and tweed.

part five:
mother lights the yellow votive candles
and places them all in a row
on the small altar
in the east corner of her bedroom.
she remembers the dead
with bits of paper
white carnations
a glass of water
one empty earthen dish
she kneels without grimacing
and does not close her eyes.
i look at her back.
she is short-waisted.
the lowest edges of her black hair
rolled under
shine almost violet.
i watch her from the doorway.
i am playing with rubber animals.
they belong to my brother.
he does not want me to have them.
few cars go by.
you can hear people talking from the street.
rising to sit on the edge of her bed
my mother dresses her hair in mourning braids
crossing them over the crown of her head.
she secures them with bobby pins
the firm touch of her palms.

she turns to look at me.
they say her eyes are light
for a woman so dark.

part six:
i carry silver coins
in the pockets of all my clothes.

photographs of my dead follow me
to each new residence.
votive candles and st. john's wort
go near the head of my grocery lists.
i burn incense
sprinkle cinnamon out the back door of my home.
a great deal of the time
i find myself looking
for no good reason
over toward the east.
i judge lovers
by the heft of mourning
below their eyes,
picking my way through their sorrows,
handling the loose stones from which they must build up
the sturdy walls of their grieving.
i forget nothing
and carry the grudges of my dead
like bowls of ash.
i have never avoided
the tombed cities i was taught to tarry in.
and i have not let my dead lie.

you might say i have
this peculiar fascination
with the dead.

✝
▪

2.

in the faubourg

Faubourg

the faubourg is a city within the larger city
and the women walk in pairs and clusters
moving along the slave-bricked streets
wearing print dresses
carrying parcels
on their hips or heads.

within the small city of the faubourg
there is always work to be done:
rooms and yards and laundry to see to
and always some trouble
to be put to rest.
burdens to be shifted
from an arm to a hip
from a hip to the head.
there are children to be scolded and sung to.
there are wares to call out
to sell or buy or search for at market.
and along the narrow banqettes leading there—
a cook
a seamstress
a day's-work-woman to find or be found.
there are chickens to feel and buy
and get their necks wrung.
palm oil to buy and sell
palm wine
hot sweet potato pies.
and there are blues to be sung or heard
above the trees and rooftops
all hours of the day and night.

the dead must be mourned and sung over
and prayers told them to carry to the other side.
the dead must be chanted and marched to their tombs
and the tombs then tended and the dogs kept away.

yatta leaves must be dried and woven into belts and baskets.
rags must be burned in sulphur to ward off mosquitoes
and slave brick crushed and scrubbed across doorways.
there is love to be made
conju to be worked.

and quiet as it is kept
most anything can be done in the faubourg.

in such a city
what name is good for a woman?
in such a city
what good is any woman's name?

Faubourg Study No. 3: The Seven Sisters of New Orleans

intro:
take me to the edge of town
there ain't nothing left for me here
i said walk me to the edge of town, baby
ain't nothing for me here no more

> *(as per the quintessential blues mama)*

1.

i do recall the day the last of them came into the city.
pack of run-down whores is what i took the lot of them for.
walking as if to come unhinged any minute,
and talking in that high-note,
that back-parish way.
was verde had to tell me
how he'd seen them
out far back as spanish fort.
give the mòn
two-three silver coins.
seemed they all were hungry
and most likely come down into the city
to pass.

well.
angelina like to died soon as she'd laid eyes on them.
pass for what? she screamed at verde,
pass for what?
just trash passing for trash
on account of a little yellow hair and tail?
got a pot to piss in nor a window to throw it out
and wanting to come downtown
trying to be something
they mòn neither they pòn
never was

course me
it was all the same to me
long as they didn't dot this doorstep.
and you might know that was just what they did.
had already got a dime or two of verde's
and then come here to me for rooms.
but that wasn't until after señorita put the lot of them out.

you should have heard all the commotion
once they took up there
living all on top one another—
which at señorita's
is the way everyone lives.
i tell you it was a mighty commotion
when señorita opened her mouth
for all the quarter to hear.
saying all how she couldn't have such carryings-on,
disturbance and strife,
in the house where she lived and worked
and ate her daily bread.
all how she just couldn't tolerate
such back-parish ways.
her place was respectable, *she said,*
no kind of cat-house.
a respectable place.
a house of assignation
on a good part of the rampart.

we later learned,
those of us who cared to know,
that the one called "baby sister"
had read señorita.
and of course señorita couldn't take it
and sent them out.
and where did they come to if not here?
right here.
and didn't even ask for verde
though he was the one helped them before.

no ma'am.
the one called belalia come straight up to the front porch
pushed the screen door to:
i'm looking for mister verde's woman
she called into the front room.
tell her i'm belalia.
one of the seven sisters.
and i'm standing in need
*of a good **clean** woman.*

2.

they were blood sisters every one of them.
grew up out in st. john's
the night the mother died
of the tumor she would not have treated
baby sister
whose given name was eulalie
took with a fit.
she made it out as far as spanish fort.
they came upon her
bleeding from the feet
from walking so far without shoe-the-first.
when they saw they could not force her to return to st. john's
they stayed with her there
and she convinced them to fast.
when the five days had come and gone
she told them not to worry.
their palms would be crossed with silver that same day.
a wagon would arrive to carry them in to new orleans.
and they would have food.
and rooms.
and not long after
verde barthelme pulled into view.

no.
they didn't come to pass or whore around.

they come to make a living
out of visions and such.
on the basis of eulalie's faith
they'd come into the city
as holy women.

3.

i swear they looked to me like any sisters might.
i'd offered them to come on in
but only belalia did.
the others stayed out on the front porch steps—
some standing
some sitting
all pressed close
around baby sister.
and when i saw up close
how she was right dark,
and one-two the others as well,
i turned my heel on all i'd thought about them,
on all angelina had been saying day-in, day-out.

those girls couldn't pass for mexican much less white.
and anyone with eyes to see would tell you
there wasn't a fast one among them.
i gave them the room verde's boy walker had died in.
i charged them a dollar and a quarter a week.
and angelina never uttered a hard word against it.

it must have been autumn or very well near it.
i remember the rains had started to come in to the city.
so it must have been early autumn
when the first one showed up
from bay st. louis
asking after a reading
with the seven sisters of new orleans.

4.

they lived on st. philip.
over there by that barthelme boy and his woman léanna.
never bothered anybody.
but then they never had to.
people came from all over.
bay st. louis.
all the way from memphis
to hear them tell
their dreams and signs.
had one called *m'dear*
she wasn't the mother of them though.
it had already been told how the mother's dying
was what sent them here in to the city in the first place.
she wasn't even the oldest.
she was the second
maybe even the third.
but they all called her that.

and the one who dreamed—
well—
they called her *baby sister.*

5.

i have heard tell of them, yes.
but i never believed the sister part.
people say they wasn't even *from* here.
come from way off somewhere.
foreigners or nations.
island people most likely.
reading and healing and getting full of spirit.
old-time hoodoo is what it sounded like to me
and i never did go in for all that.
roots and chamy bags and carryings-on.
and how come it's always got to be some *negro* woman

43

got to heal everybody?
what kind of colored woman *did you* ever meet
had time or inclination
to sit on a chair all day
dreaming and healing?
me, i had to work too hard.
and when i'm done over to the factory of an evening
them days i had children to raise.
had a man to feed.
had me a plot of ground i used to work out there in back.
yes ma'am.
misbelieve, collards, banana,
date palm,
melon here and there,
tomato,
sweet bell pepper.
even had a few camellia bushes out front the steps.
saturdays i baked all day
and sunday was mass and visiting the ailing and the dying
and supper for minor's people come noon.
and monday come another week all over again
and full-up with white folk besides.
no ma'am.
i never had time for no hoodoo.
and *seven* in one family and sisters too?
seven women all sitting on chairs
healing people from detroit and the west coast.

6.

going down into the city, baby
leaving it all far far behind me
i'm going down into the big city, baby
gonna leave all y'all behind
gettin' out before this mis'ry
make me up and lose my mind
i said i'm gone

7.

hail mary full of grace
         érzulie, mother of women
blessèd art thou
         there is truth to be made here
blessèd art thou
         dreams, mother, to be dreamt
blessèd art thou
         visions to be told
blessèd mother
         o!   lead me to the pathway
blessèd mother
         over the barred footing
holy holy
         érzulie
                   érzulie
         mother

mother
         mother of women

8.

lizette,
aurélie;
marie-claude named for father,
anne-louise, the blackest among us,
belalia who speaks for baby sister,
and my name is albertine
whom the sisters call m'dear,
and eulalie—
baby sister—
also dark,
who tells dreams and signs
gives out sayings and readings
but only when she must.
and only for the mother.

9.

you might not be from here.
but one time
some of your people
had to be from the city.
that's how we call new orleans, you know.
the city.
only city hereabouts.
some people think it's the only city worth knowing,
how would we know though?
we never go too far away.
no need to.
sooner or later
everyone comes to the city.
it's an old saying.

yes, daughter.
your people would have been from just over in tremé.
else you never would have got so far
packing that camera and your satchel of questions.
people round these parts don't tell much.
never did.
but you've got that look.
and that's the only reason they sent you here to me.
oh yes.
people'll fill you full of good food round our way.
and talk to you till you drop.
keep you all kinds of company—
but no one sends you to mother josefina
because of any of that.
and no one tells a *thing*
that is not for you to know.
so never mind about your questions
and just let me see what-all i might tell you:
i might tell you things you don't need or even want to hear.
i might tell you about your people over this way.
like i might tell you your condition.

but, daughter
let mother josefina tell you this one thing:
as long as you are here in the city
and whatever else you do
just don't you dream that journey.

10.

kind words
a place to stay
good company among neighbors who watch and report
and seemingly never intrude
(and more food than anyone *living* can eat)
their hospitality is a way of teaching strangers
to know their place
a way of protecting the history
from falling into the wrong hands.
but you can not go without learning much
when you are not the stranger
you have so counted on being,
when you are really returning home.
you see too much; you feel too much
and you are always compelled to ask after even more.

the next thing, of course is you begin to dream—
that much i knew almost from the start.

11.

there is much i could tell you, daughter.
but none of it would satisfy your need to know.
i could tell you they died one after the other
the way ordinary people do.
i could tell you they passed into some vision of baby sister's.
i could tell of the long train of men and women
black, white, foreigners from i-don't-know-where
who beat their paths to this door

one after the other
looking for the sign
to fix their souls
or put their lives at peace
to heal their bodies or return some lost prize.
i could tell you how they changed my life,
the things i saw
or hoped or thought or dreamt i saw
the days i kept their company
scrubbing the floor where baby sister stood and walked
as she gave out
what few words she ever spoke aloud.
and i was glad to be of use.
a child
sent here by my father
because my mother died after birthing me
with the veil across my eyes.
he didn't have much learning,
god rest his poor country soul.
but he'd given me everything else,
schooling,
good clothes,
what love he had left, for mama's sake.
so then he gave me the possibility
of the nearness to the journey.
oh yes.
there is so much you might learn from me.
all how i came to live in this house.
the house of the seven sisters.
though all this is not it.
the old house burnt almost down.
i saved what i could.
an altar setting caught afire
burnt away a good part of the chapel.
i saved some things.
that's how i come to be as you see me now—
saving and setting aside

so much that could have been lost.
and what you *see* here
is nothing.
as i said, i was a girl.
no more than a servant
and glad to be that.
glad to be of use.
oh, the many ways i was of use,
and to baby sister.
so much that the others never trusted me.
only m'dear had a kind word for me.
"baby sister wants you now" she said to me.
and i stopped all or whatever i was doing
and went into the chapelroom.
she was a girl, you understand.
like me.
she was just a girl without a mother,
just a little older than i was then.
you'd think they'd've understood, being her sisters,
and all so much older.
but no.
only m'dear knew or cared to know.
"it's time" m'dear said,
her voice like shallow water.
"baby sister wants you now"

that was how it was.

it was me she wanted to touch.
she believed i could feel what she felt, you see.
i was just a motherless child my own self.
only way i knew to be.
only life i knew was me and papa and saturday mass before her.
and you know, daughter,
it's true what they say:
a womanchild without her mother journeys a far piece of road.
the old folk say it

and i tell you it is true.
so it was me and baby sister.
me and eulalie.

i used to sing to her
songs she taught me from her mother—
which, i never did know.
yes.
i sang to her so that we could be girls together.
and more than girls.

and she used to read my dreams
"dream for me," she used to plead when i would go.
"dream for me tonight, josefina."
what could i do?
could i lie to her?
when we were girls like that together?
or else pretend some other dream?
no.
she wept like her heart was breaking that one day, daughter.
she wept so hard i wept along with her.
she walked the floor weeping
and me holding her up and weeping my own self.
because we both knew i had dreamt that dream, you see.

look.

> *oh mother i am on the pathway*
> *oh mother i am on the road*
> *oh mother i am on the pathway*
> *oh mother i am on that road*
> > *shallow water*
> > *shallow water loa-mama*
> > *shallow water loa-mama*
>
> *érzulie*
> *érzulie*

mother
    where i find my mother
        along the shallow shallow water

the rains are coming in to the city
in no more than a week.
it never did take much of a rain to flood these narrow
streets.

but can you say it?
can you look at me, daughter
and say you have not dreamt that journey?
'course you can't.
come over closer, baby.
come where mother can touch you.

12.

oh it come up a mighty rain
and it blowed my house away
i said it come up a mighty rain
just blowed all my house away
couldn't find no place to please me
so i ride this lonesome train

13.

it has been three years.
and i have put away my satchel and my camera.
what notions i had
for some authentic study
some record of their lives.

the only family i have in the city
is uncle walker's granddaughter ava lee.

she sings at a new club on the rampart,
ANYBODY'S PLACE.

i will not seal or rent or close off any of this house.
and i do not lock doors.
i live among the sacred objects of their lives:
lizette, aurélie, marie-claude named for their father,
belalia who spoke for baby sister and bore her grudges,
anne-louise the blackest among them.
albertine whom the sisters called m'dear,
who organized their days,
who sought out josefina from her father's house
while she was still a child,
and baby sister: eulalie,
who on the basis of one solitary journey
made a living for them all
out of dreams and signs,
and died of clearly natural causes
at fourteen or fifteen or sixteen years old.

i live here.
i see few people
except for the handful of elderly neighbors
who still come to tell me their remembrance.
i listen to them all
recalling in single portions
josefina,
the things she told me
and her way of telling,
her early warning, still too late—
for me—
that song she broke into
of pathways and crossings,
ava lee
who consigns us all to the blues
impromptu
and unrecorded.

but i keep my own counsel
and i touch nothing
no one:

i want to walk a little farther
along the shallow water
i want to live a little longer
with my dangerous dream

The Evening News
(a letter to Nina Simone)

a wail
a whoop
a line brought back from nowhere.
deep violet of memory,
stored up against hard times' coming.
we were righteous then,
experienced in things we had not seen
but always knew
would pass this way.

we had righteousness on our side.

they say you stood before a small audience in
new orleans last year and abused them for their smallness.
not just their numbers
but their looks.
their soulless way of sitting
and waiting to be entertained.
they told me how you stood there and cursed them good.
told me how they took it
for the sake
of all they used to be so long ago they never could forget.
could only say like the old folk, when cornered perhaps,
said *"i disremember"*

i asked them what you wore.

i remembered the years i struggled with the very private fear
that i would remain a child forever
and miss all that was major in our one moment of glory.
even a child knows there is one such moment.
one.

even i had sense enough to see you and not weep.
even a child then understood the words
"sister"
"brother"
"people"
"power"

and anyone could see we were all the evening news.

and hear you sing—
at least that was what they called it.
it was my best girlfriend's sister
who came up on us closed off in her bedroom
laughing over her cosmetics, her jewelry, her sex, her t.v.
and instead of sending us out
leaned there in the doorway and smiled.
"you two know so much,
want to be so grown and everything,
need to quit all that giggling
and learn to listen to nina."
that was late autumn.
aletha came into her own bedroom and sat between us on the
bed.
she turned up the volume
but did not change the station.
we watched her and her college friends
in dashikis and afros
on the evening news.

that year marceline and i listened close
to the lyrics and the ways
the easy breaths and breathless lines
the underground silences
of you and roberta.
we argued and sassed,

slapped hands on our hips at the slightest provocation,
and learned when and when not to apologize for it.
two brown girls acting out,
mothers looking out over our heads that way they had then
whenever we went so far we did not need to be told.
we gave our telephone numbers to those boys
with the hippest walks
the better grade of afro
the deep-changing voices,
and we never took their calls.
we danced the sophisticated sissy
the thing
the shake
the go-on
the soul strut.
we counted our girlfriends
"soul sister number 1"
"soul sister number 2."
marceline learned to cornrow
and i braided my older brother's bush each night.
we were too much and we knew it.
we thought we understood it all.

deep violet
deep violet

but that was years ago.
and you were in your glory then.

then,
while i was still younger than i knew or admitted,
and studying in the south of france,
i danced four nights out of five and all weekend,
my arms on the hips or shoulders
of some wiry brother from cameroun or ivory coast
senegal, algeria, panama, martinique,

one of only six or seven young black women at uni-
versity
among the dozens and dozens of dark men who cir-
cled us
weaving their weightless cloth
their heavy guard.
escorted when i would have been alone
fed when i had no hunger
driven when i lacked a destination
protected from the mere possibility of danger—
and danger to them
we knew
meant "frenchmen/
whitemen"—
courted and cosseted
and danced into sleeplessness.
"you will be old one day, sister.
then, you will sleep fine."
but their hearts,
the dark wiry hearts of the brothers,
were in the right places.

the foolish ones said
"you are like women of my country"
and feigned weaknesses no one would believe
they ever even remotely had known.
and often enough
had the immediate good sense
to laugh at themselves
and grin at the rest of us.
the others did something like waiting,
danced endlessly, and at the end of evening said
"i have this sister,
this nina.
play some for my sister here, man.
man, get up and put on that nina simone."

and we sat in the silence in the dark
as one found the shiny vinyl
and put the needle to the darker groove.
we sat choked with roman cigarettes
too much dancing
too much good food.
we sat listening and did not touch.
we looked at one another's hands
and read recognition there.
one day we would be old.
we would sleep
and no longer know one another.
we sat into the night
until we grew hungry again and sick from the stale air.
we listened
we wailed
we did not touch
or bow down our heads.

and that is the meaning
of the word *expatriate.*

if you live right
if you live right
if you live right

but what has living done for you?

i heard your voice
over the radio late one night in cambridge
telling how you never meant to sing.
whoever interviewed you hardly said a word.
he asked his questions
and you took your time.
you breathed long breaths between phrases,
your speaking voice lighter

and less lived in than i remembered.
you sang a line or two
and talked about your "life."
i asked my question
directly into the speaker—
"what the hell did living do for you, girl?"
i sat on the floor and drank my coffee.
i paced the carpet between your pauses.
i pulled my nightdress up in both hands and danced.
but i got no satisfaction that night.
and, for what it matters,
heaven did not come to me either.

don't talk to me about soul.
don't tell me about *no* damned soul.
years and years and years
of *all night long*
and-a where are you
and making time and doing right.
expatriate years.
years, woman, years.
where *were* you?

and then you sang "Fodder on My Wings"
with not a note of holy in your voice,
and what could i do?
a young woman,
i put myself to bed.

it was the following year
that you cursed them down in new orleans.
dragged for them like muddy water.
i listened to the story on the telephone
or looked into the faces i came on in the streets.
"what"
i asked them

"did she wear?"
and do you think they could tell me?
all i asked the people
was *what did the woman have on?*

and what about it?
if your country's full of lies
if your man leaves you
if your lover dies
if you lose your ground and there is no higher ground
if your people leave you
if you *got* no people
if your pride is hurting
if you got no pride, no soul
if you living in danger
if you living in mississippi, baltimore, detroit
if you walk right, talk right, pray right
if you don't bow down
if you hungry
if you old
if you just don't know
please
please
outside-a you there is no/
place to / go
these are the expatriate years, these.
what is left.

the people dragged their sorry asses out to see you
and you cursed them
and you looked out into their faces, those you could see
and accused them
you called them down for all those years.
you sang the songs you sang when you were younger

and you made them pay.

and then
deep violet
and a longer time no one will speak of.

dear nina,
i want to say to you how we did not mean it.
how we did not mean to give you up
to let you go off alone that way.
i want to say how we were a younger people, all of us.
but none of it is true.
we used you
and we tossed what we could not use to the whites
and they were glad to get it.
we tossed you out into such danger
and closed our eyes and ears to what was to become of you
in those years—
deep
deep violet—
and worst of all
we did not even say your name.
we ate you like good hot bread
fresh from the table of an older woman
and then we tossed the rest out for the scavengers.
does it matter?
does it matter when and how we did it to you?
does it matter we got no righteousness from it?
that we felt no shame?
does it matter we took all good things in excess then,
and then again?
not only you
but all things?
does it matter we sometimes return to you now,
in the back rooms of childhood friends,
forgiven lovers?
does it matter this is no gift or tribute or right or holy thing
but just a kind of telling

a chronicle to play back
against those images that never quite made it
to the evening news?

how cursed,
how sorry a mess of people can we be, nina
when outside-a you
there is no place
to go?

Note: The line "heaven did not come to me either" is based on the
song "If You Pray Right (Heaven Belongs to You)," by Nina Simone.
The lines "outside-a you / there is no / place to go" are from Andy
Stroud's "Be My Husband," as sung by Nina Simone.

Speaking of Trains

for Moses Nkondo

South Train Study, Movement 1

in the early morning hours
when the building makes what few sounds it has rehearsed
during my brief sleep or absence
i move about
as little and as cautiously as possible
among strewn books and record jackets—
lyrics that tell of train whistles
of men standing alone
in vacant lots
men in the process of leaving cleveland
st. louis, d.c.
trains heading south into the night
trains that never return.
i toy with phrases like
cultural memory
canonization of despair—
i invoke rituals of loss and forgetting.

i do not sing.

i make this other sound
that catches the tissue of my throat like a bit of fishbone:
it dries there
and returns
in chorus with some country harmonica or bass guitar
a piano touched
by rude eloquent hands.
and i feel at the pit of my belly
the most critical essay of my career:

this year
i interrogate the blues.

going down to the river / gonna take my own
easy chair / and if the blues don't get me /
i'm gonna rock right on away from here /
that's why . . .

infra-blue:
ritual study in struggle.
i interrogate the blues
for something like fullness of meaning—
but there are codes here
dark men
and darker women—
and i feel in my own hands
the immeasurable buoyancy
of *am i blue?*
am i blue?

went down to the railroad / laid my head
down on that track / got to thinking 'bout
my woman / snatched my devilish head back /
wanna know how long . . .

in a new york barbershop-headshop
the older brothers talk trash
incorporate me into rituals
of loss and suffocation
desire and claim checks and umbrella stands
razor cut
trim-and-shave
pomade:

"what was her name?"

"man, i never did know.
but she only ever wore blue.

hell.

i just called her baby."

st. louis, chicago, d.c.
and the men stand vacant in their lots
in the process of memorizing
canonizing some moment.

> *in the dark / in the dark / baby, you and me /*
> *in the dark /*

like any other sensible man
i carry home that image
like i carry home my haircut—
incognito.
absolutely prepared
to promise things i cannot possibly give
if i can know her name
if i can know how she got away that way
in the dark.

i interrogate my senses
for the dark woman coded in blue.
like any sensible man
i work my way through traffic to the station.
she does not arrive.
evening trains
never do arrive.
i change my mind.
forget this city.
which of these women could ever remember?
which of these women
could be movement in blue?

it is evening.
i have my fishbone
and my hands on my belly.
i have my essay

and my evening meal.
i move about as little as possible.
the older brothers
and their infra-blue.
railway stations south to cities i will never see.
i have my ritual study in struggle-in-the-dark.
i have my dark code
painted onto the backs of my hands.
i practice
how i will say

"some questions
have more rhythm than others"

> *repeat*
> *repeat*
> *offstage/enter woman in blue.*

Movement 2: How to Meet the Train

i have a method
for meeting the train
no one has scooped.
i go with empty hands.
i go with my beard
just barely unkempt.
i stand apart from the wall—
never lean.
i do not smoke
or drink
or eat the salted nuts.
i have a method for meeting the train
no one has scooped.

missing trains all my life
at one station or another
i have become

a man who understands
the cries of whistles—
the process of waiting.

going to meet the train
i wear my city eyes
turn up my collar
uncautious—
still not reckless.
distant—
but not yet incognito.
you think you recognize me.
but oh the many ways i could tell you you are wrong.

Incognito: Woman in Blue

the streets are empty tonight.
i walk alone along this evening street
carrying nothing.
i have business in this street
i will divulge to no one.
i have some place in your dead remembrances
and i will not set you free.
you may not touch me
or speak to me
or discover my name.
i have these gifts for you.
you must accept them
without ever discerning
what they might be.

it is a hard business we bargain in here tonight.
and there is strange conju afoot,
brother.

("incognito—
woman in blue

walks—
past every known landmark
past every familiar thing
by which i might know her.
she does not stop
or change pace.
she does not look back.
she walks as if she had no hips
nor anything between them—
as if she had
no concept
of mercy.

in the distance
inside some one of these houses
someone is trying
to sing like sarah vaughan.
it is not raining.")

these might be any streets
we might find ourselves
in any of a dozen lonely, yellow-lit cities.
we might be kin or lovers
or any other sorry strangers
in any foolish, terrible time.
and around us,
the night,
the dark,
and the hungry yellow street lights.
watch your step,
brother.
remember:
i know who you are.
watch your step.
negro men in every time
negro men better and wiser and lovelier than you
have been known to lose

life and the dream of life
in safer streets than these

and just ahead
is the station.

Elvena

1.

there is a house down on old roman street
all the women pass through.
one stands outside the gate
bare feet
broad skirts gathered loosely
about her hips.
have you lost anything today?
tell me, neighbor
what have you lost today?
and her madness is a conju
slung like rope about the heart.
i said i feel her madness like a conju
like a rope
slung round my heart.

do you see elvena?
she got that way touching neighbor-women
on the edges of their fingers.
do you see that bone-step walk she walks?
and the women who go by
looking past her face
past the ash-black hands
pretending they do not see her
and nothing has been lost?
a woman can go so far out
there never will be a way back.
and there are things a woman will do
can't be learned
and won't be understood.
but somebody's got to be a witness.
don't tell me you don't see that woman
moving barefoot along the banqette.

70

2.

a woman goes barefoot along the banqette this evening.
no one speaks her name.
the neighbor-people have difficulty recalling her—
and no one ever remembers a woman
as she once was

there is a neighbor-woman out there
a long ways from shoring
throw out your shimmy straps
and roll that woman in

who will touch her now?
who?
the mothers with their prayer-bands
wound tight about their wrists and waists?
the widows stabbing bricked pavements
with their low-heeled shoes,
little beads of sweat just visible above the lips,
the pearls of mourning strung effortless across their bosoms?
maybe the younger sisters she taught so well,
the school-girls who skip and prance with ease?
or else the ones riding by
on hips a man would shout over?
a neighbor-woman stands outside the gate this evening.
somebody's got to be a witness
somebody ought to call her name

3.

i used to be a woman other people called by name.
lived in a house
where the blues clung to the ceilings
to all the doors and the side-porch
and all around my garden

out back of the house.
i used to go to that garden
and sing all the blues i could find.
you'd be surprised how much blues can grow
between the hidden-lily and the monkey-grass
overnight.

the man next door
was from somewhere out in the country.
was making a kind of cloth.
worked at it all the time.
i would see him standing back in the shadows.
i could tell he was listening
and sometimes i thought he said my name—
as if it meant something.
he never did.
just stood there in the shadows
working that cloth
and listening to my blues.
sometimes i wondered
what kind of blues
that man had learned to make or give.
and sometimes i wondered
if he put my song into that cloth.
and what he might have lost besides.

and tell me, neighbor
what have you lost today?

4.

only the bone-step women
would ever come for her in broad daylight
carrying their satchels of longing
like easy parcels on turbaned heads.
carrying that woman along
between the folds of their red cotton skirts

calling aloud, to no one in particular
tell the truth
tell the truth and do right
carrying that woman along like one more burden
one more parcel
that amounts to nothing much
moving along the broken road
that leads to bayou st. john.

elvena could walk among them
bare feet keeping time
to the bones up on their heads.
tell the truth, i could hear them shout.
tell the truth and do right
i know you are a witness
just tell the truth and do right

5.

the bone-step women do not come.
i sit on my front-porch into the night.
i am working colored cloth
from cuts of used string.
i see elvena when she steps down from the banqette.
i see her step
into the empty street
ash-black hands turned out
palms facing toward me.
i hold up the unfinished cloth-piece
and she begins to sing:

tell me, neighbor
what that blues is made from
tell me
tell me
i want to know
what have you lost today?

Everything Happens to (Monk and) Me
for J. B. Borders IV

we hustle hard as the rest of the folk me and my baby
but it never seems to count.
so
we stop off nights and hear the best and worst of everybody.
my baby's down in heart but that hasn't stopped him yet.
me i'm just down.
we struggle-in.
we sit ourselves down.
we believe in everything.
we know the other life is a club called havana.
we dream in unison how it will be there
and have never had this conversation because we do not need
    to.
we believe in everything my baby and me.
we *know* that life on the other side is a club called havana
and sometimes we ache for it
but not out loud.

the music in this city is not heard in clubs.
this is not a thing we recite
we know this
by heart.
no.
it's in the thrumming of the empty streetcar tracks
the thrumming of the old wooden banqettes beneath the
    newer cement
it's in the bricks the slaves are cursing over eternally
the way the poorest of the crazies look up from rheumy eyes
the way a workingman hauls his haunches home to his woman
a little low on one side his walk
a little bit too hurried or too slow
for him for her one
the way she doesn't wait but puts his plate over water
pretending to watch the news

washing her hands
or else not stirring
pretending not to daydream
over porkchops and brown gravy

the thrumming is in the way it hangs
the whole city hanging
at the edge of a water no one will wade
the whole city hanging
the way the not-so-young-anymore men used to say
"can you *hang* with that?" and mean it
mean it.
that's the problem with this city
we *all* mean it so hard.
and this is a soft city
a city of softness
turning turning ever on the edge of its own meaning
and hanging on to *us* for dear life.
we really
really
mean
to get it right soon some glorious day some soft thrumming
    night
and "oh" cry out the pretty little street-stepping-boys some-
    times
"ain't we righteous, y'all!"
yes sweetness we mouth in their direction when we hear or see
    or care
we really truly are

and that's what started the whole damn thing to begin with:

me and my baby just want to hear some music from time to
    time.
well i do.
my baby he loves me and sometimes just says okay.
and sometimes he just fakes it like he doesn't have this longing.

my baby thinks he's stoic—
that old negro stoicism sterling loved so.
but no
he wouldn't be so sad around the eyes late evening into
    night
after supper and before cigarettes
—we still have supper here
and late-night breakfast
and say "good evening" after twelve noon—
he wouldn't have those *eyes*
not from being old-fashioned sterling/negro-stoic
oh-but-no we say here (first syllable stressing)
truth is he's old-fashioned negro-martyr heroic.
i get him.
then i get him out.
we get out into or behind the crowd.
we do not need to look at one another
we nod
we hang our hands about as if we've known it all along.
we thrum
we thrum
we thrum
inside the city

at least that's how it is
when we condescend to our hipper selves

"oh baby" we say together later on
"oh
oh, baby"

but ain't we righteous y'all?

and out of nowhere in the night
solo
standards
the funny-sad

the halved
the tired
witty
unlovely chords
and everything within us that ever hoped for hipness
    stirs.
not following that sound
we laugh into the night
because we were young once
and very very hip.
we were young once
and very very wise.
we were young once
these streets were always ours
we paved them with the flats of our heels
we danced
and never bothered to tire
or if we did it hardly mattered
our hippest coolest livest selves
out late and full up with heart
valiant as the very streets
we wind we wind me and my baby
we reach the other side the place called havana
we reach our own unlovely selves
—bitter chords—
reach for each other
and are wise
enough to know better
our tender places older than before.

it never ends.
we follow the sweep of the river downtown and up.
somewhere is music we can hear
havana and unlovely chords
and right here with us
the city and the indigo night
its tuneless keyboard silent altogether for the moment

we play upon the night
each key a treasure we have close-*tight* between us
unrighteous
and unlovely
full up with longing
in the streets.

3.

ex votos

Mother Catherine

my name is catherine.
some call me mother
some saint.

and do you claim sainthood?
do you admit to having duped
       these poor ignorant negroes
       into believing you are holy?
       into building your likeness into a statue
       and then closeting this statue away
       because it is, like you,
       a holy thing?

well.
i admit they often call me saint.
and yes, there is a statue.
and yes
anyone looking can see
       i
       like my followers
       am negro.

(laughter)

besides
those two there
the ones you point to
—it is not a good thing to point, you know, my child?—
those two may well be poor
but they have prospered by me in the past.
and they are white men's negroes anyway to come here.
and so their fate is sealed.

(murmuring
shifting of chairs and of feet)

still
there are others—
a hundred or more—
who bow before you
and call you sainted.

yes.
and i bow to them all.
i can bow to all of you.
what harm is done?
is this your idea, my child
of the evil in me?
well.
i am not young anymore
so let me save you a bit of time.
there is a statue.
there is also a chapel made all in stone.
the statue of course sits in the chapel.
                    (more laughter)
and also the people
          —all of them negroes like me.
and quite a few, i suppose
like those two sitting there.
and do you know
do you have any idea what it is that happens in my chapel
with me
and my statue
and my negroes?
we stand.
we kneel.
sometimes we faint.
negroes do faint you know
          but only on special occasions
(uproarious laughter)
sometimes we sing
or else we chant or speak in tongues.
sometimes when the spirit moves us so

we dance.

aha! there!
dancing in chapel!
can this be any but the work of the very devil?
of the old foe?
satan himself?

(outcries
and stamping of feet)

carry off this woman
this negress
from this blessèd congress.
set her to some proper labor
something fitting for her age and temperament.

and the statue?

leave it there
locked as it is in its stone room.
we can not have her followers
forever banging at the gates of heaven crying for justice.
they are negroes, remember.
it is one of the few words they all
                    can say and write as well in every language.
let them keep their stone statue.
a generation or so
and they will soon forget.

(quiet
        hush)

and so you find me—
not even a man's socks and slippers
and only a white dimity on my head.
they used to have me drawing up their holy water.

but now i am a common lavatrice.
i wash their robes.
and that is why
whenever it rains and thunders and pours there in the lower nine
and floods the levees
my followers
those who remember me can be heard saying:
"it is mother catherine
washing the robes of the blessèd congress of the saints
and showering down her blessings on her people."

St. Martin

o little slave saint with your broom of pampas and your cross
pray for us your little brothers and sisters driven like cattle to
    the market.
little saint of lima
remember your mother's own labors and what she paid for
    your freedom.
remember
remember
benísimo negrito santo:
you who were spared the labor of the fields
negrito santo:
spared by your white father's whims and taken off to far
    ecuador
negrito santo:
given as so much fodder to the hungriness of the fat pale
    monks.
they say you are sainted.
they say you are holy.
they say you are merciful, pious, good.
they say that you gave to eat to the very rats of lima and for
    this

                you were made holy in the sight of heaven.
but we see you ever with your little broom of pampas
and we know they have sent you to sweep the floors of their
    heaven.
even so, little saint
negrito santo
we pray to your broom of pampas and your wooden cross:
remember, remember, remember
that we your brothers and sisters are not spared.
benísimo san martin de porres
slave of all saints
pray for us.
san martin de porres
benísimo

pray for us that all our labors are not in vain.
o little black brother with your broom and your cross and
    your
            eyes lifted up
we labor and are wasted away
while you stand sweeping in the big house and are spared.
little saint
hermano nostro
where is your mercy now, where is your pity, your goodness
all your love of the poor?
o negrito santo de dios
can you not put down your broom for even one minute and
    answer us?
st. martin:
forgive us if we are impatient but the sun beats hot down here
    in
            our fields.
st. martin:
forgive us if we have not enough patience but we fear we are
    forgotten down here.
st. martin:
who are you to ignore us when your own mother—
blessèd morena, madre dos pobrecitos—
your own mother labored among us (until the great don
    returned
and elevated her from slave-girl to servant)
forgive us st. martin of the broom and the cross.
forgive us if we have sinned.
forgive us because you know that you yourself sinned mightily
when you took on their white robes and their heaven
for the price of a meal.
we are not an evil race, martin
but a tortured one.
nor do we forget the many ways of torture.
remember
little black saint:
the day of the drum is yet to come.

remember benísimo:
that the ancestors do not die.
remember
benísimo negrito santo:
the price of your mother's shoes and your own flowing robes.
and pray for us so that we may be delivered of this travail
and that when we go finally to speak our little piece
we can say, "bless also our brother martin
who prayed us out from a terrible sojourn in a terrible
    kingdom
for the love of an ever more terrible king."
benísimo negrito santo
take up your broom and sweep confusion into the eyes of
    those other saints.

cross out our suffering and the chains that bear down our lives.
and do not forget us.
benísimo
esclavo
dos santos.
amen.

✝

Sor Juana

santísima sor juana
hija de madre morena
sor de san martin
little virgin with your feet of gold
i hear your cries
and my poor troubles pale before your own.
santísima corazón de piedad
i see you
    before the gates of heaven where you stand unable to enter in
    because your bruised and battered body can carry you no farther
    and the other saints
    with their rosaries and their white hands of clay
    do not stoop to help you in this your final disgrace.
    they say that they are proper saints.
    they say they are sorry for your suffering
    sorry it is not enough in the eyes of their holy mother church
    to make you one among them for all your pain.
    and behind the high gates of san pedro
    they call you heretic
    worker of black forces
    mulata.

i see you, sor juana
and in my lowered soul
equal parts of humility and shame:
humility for the pettiness of my own day-to-day existence
and shame for my forebears
those of my race and thus my own blood
who stoned you to death
    on the path to the cursèd cambio dos negros of espíritu santo
who slaughtered you as a goat before the eyes
    of the very whites who loathed you so
or was it fear, in the end,
that made them send one of your own

to spread the evil word
  that you were in league with the white masters
who said you betrayed us
and who stoned you there in the evil market of our shame
knowing you did not?
shame, sor juana
for ever do i hear you crying in the streets of espíritu santo:
"oye! oye, merditos!
stop
stop, you fools
i am the sister of martin de porres!"

o santísima juanita
it is one hundred years
it is two hundred years
and still we labor.
is there no word we can say
no petition we can make
no offering we can offer up to expiate the great sin of our fathers?
juanita
santísima
batardita santa
it is true our forebears sinned against you
  and against the great god.
it is true that we are their children
  and so must share in their eternal damnation.
take our lives
our life's blood
the children from our wombs that drop into the fields
  of this cursèd land we slave in.
see our devotion to your sainted brother
  san martin de porres
  born of your same mother
  and patron of such battered poor
  as we who call on you now
  for forgiveness
  and the freedom that our fathers never knew.

juanita
santísima
is eternity so long as this?
juanita
santísima
we the faithful press our lips to your golden feet
juanita dorada
expiate the sins of our ancestors which have fallen upon us.
here is sugar
barley, coffee, gold
the forbidden coca of the gods of the forests
how can we repay you, juanita?
where does all our blood go
    when it spills into the white man's fields?
juanita santísima
juanita dorada
o wronged one o martyred one
how long can your eternity last?

the year is 1818, juanita
and there is talk of independence
in the streets
and across the great sertão
is it your desire, little sister
to free us of the bonds your mother wore in her shame?
is it your plan juanita santísima
to pardon our forebears and we who pay ever more dearly
    for their wrongs against you?
or shall we be slaughtered
    on the floors of espíritu santo, little sister
    and driven into the dust wherefrom we call on your holy name?
we are black and poor and despised
even so, juanita
we know that independence is a white man's word.
will you stand for the whites to be freed of their masters who live
    across the seas
and leave us

your cursèd ones
to serve them ever in our shame, our tortured
    memories of the fate inflicted on you?

the year is 1828, juanita
and there is talk of war with ecuador
in the streets
and across the great sertão.
is it your desire, little sister
. . .

the year is 1839, juanita
and there is talk of invasion from angry chile, little sister.
they talk this in the streets
and across the great sertão
what is your plan, juanita
for the faithful among us?
. . .

the year is 1861,
. . .
it is 1895,
1930, '45
. . .
eternity, eternity, eternity,
what are the wars, the woes
    the petty battles of the whites who control our destiny
    ever since you cursed us in your dying breath
    that we would forever labor so among them
    never knowing our right hand from our left
    tortured
    and confused
    maddened by your own doom.

sor juana
juanita

santísima
thy tortured golden body is ever before our eyes.

sor juana
juanita
we the faithful do not forget.
we recall that in 1759
one hundred years
after your sainted death on the cursèd streets of espíritu santo
hundreds of thousands of our brothers and sisters
unable to expiate the sins of our fathers
left the plantations of the nearby callāo
of arequipa
some say even quito, across the border, on the coast
but mostly here in cursèd lima
they left the plantations
they left the canefields,
the wheat, the barley, the coffee
they left the rice, the corn
even the potatoes
   (earth's own apples)
they left the lard, the cotton, the dried meat plants
so confused
so turned aside were they
by their lives of endless toil, some say.
but we
   (your faithful)
we know better, juanita.
we know it was you
your final words
we know they heard you crying
in your round golden voice:
"have pity
oye, merditos
i am the sister
of martin de porres."
we know how you called them to the great great ocean

we know how you tempted them
    with the soil of africa which you carried beneath your tongue
o pobrecita!
we know you called them to the water's edge
held out the soil of our africa in your bruised left hand
and walked them into the waters where they drowned.

sor juana
some called it madness
but we your faithful
know it was not so.
and so we come to you
and we no longer say the year.
why should you care, dorada
stopped as you are at the very gates of their heaven?
we come to you in a latter day ritual.
we choose from among our own
the purest
the sweetest
the most faithful of our own young daughters.
and we do not forget, santísima.
we do not forget that on that wretched day
    when they took you from us forever
that three or four of those who did not believe it
who gave no credit to the white priests' lies
who knew that you
    holy woman that you were and gifted
knew that it was their way to kill two birds with one stone:
to put down the insurrection of our fathers
and also the cries of the slaves and even from among the free blacks
that you, juanita
santísima
sister of martin de porres
because of your gifts of healing and of tongues and so much else
be sainted then and there in your own lifetime.
then it was that a group of your followers
    (sainted women every one)

took up your body and carried it home through the streets
crying and beating bared breasts
and rubbing your blood and tears into their flesh.
we have not forgotten how
when they had disrobed your battered golden body
they prayed in the old tongue over all your parts
rubbing the places
where every cut and bruise and bloody scar stood out.
we are faithful, dorada
and do not forget.

and so it is, sor juana
remembering your holy travail at the hands of your own people
we choose from among
the sweetest
the cleanest
the purest of our own virgin daughters
she who is most like you.
we take her into the open courtyard.
and the first stones we give to her mother
her sisters
the sisters of her mother.
the rest among us, as we are able,
we take up the other stones.
we know she is but a child and so
we grasp the stones of our evil close to our palms
we do not loose them.
we take up the instruments
of our evil
our betrayal.
mother and sisters first
we strike
we weep
we call her by your holy name:
"juanita
juanita
santísima sor de martin de porres

pardon us for the evil we inflict upon you
pardon us for the sins of our mothers and fathers
pardon the betrayal of our slave ancestors who took your life
juanita
juanita
we are altogether filthy
cleanse us with your blood turned to attar of roses
o saint
o holy
o perfect child without sin"
we call her by your holy name
and then we pray that the evil we have done
and the prayers that we have spoken
be turned to our good
and the good of our children
and the children of our children.
we recall, juanita
how in those last moments
after they had bathed you with the oil of roses
how your aged, battered skin
turned once more golden
healed
made young again and virgin before the eyes of your holy women.
we remember, juanita
and we pray for expiation
and your blessing.
and sometimes she is restored to us
the little saint named in your honor.
and sometimes she is not.
sometimes she wakens
pure and fresh, her skin soft and supple without equal.
and sometimes not.
sometimes our prayers are no good.
sometimes you take no faith in our paltry words and deeds.
and when that is the case
we buy white laces for the mother and the sisters.
we say to them

that it was but a little life.
we say that you sometimes grow lonely
    there on your stoop at the gates of heaven.
that you
    restored as you were in death to your own virgin girlhood
    are become again a lonely little girl
    taken by the rich don
    from the loving arms of a slave mother.
    that every now and then
    you claim one of our little girls
    to come and play in the sand
    there at the gates of heaven.
we buy white laces for the mother and the sisters.
we set them up in mourning
and offer up sugar
coffee and gold
we dress them out in roses
the white roses of death and expiation
we say such children are perfect and without sin
called as they are
to sit with you for eternity
beneath the gates of san pedro's heaven.
we say it is a chancy
and a necessary rite.
we say that generations will be forgiven
set free
made clean.
but we know it is not enough.

is it your desire, little sister?
your plan?
how long is eternity, juanita?

hija de madre morena.
santísima sor de san martin
santísima sor juana

with your wounds and your roses
and your battered skin restored to youthful gold
mulata benita.
juanita.

✝
▪

amen.

The Head of Luís Congo Speaks

1720

congo, tiamca, colango, matinga
bambara, nago
senegal, creole
i am the head of luís congo
and i speak for him
lying
burnt and rotting in some farmer's field.
and you
you may chant and shout
and dance about your bonfires on the levees.
and drink your aguardiente till you burst.
drink up until your eyes shine liquid.
and you will never have the vision that he had.
will never see the world as he saw.
what are you in the end
            but a wretched lot of slaves?
the lot of you
slaves
in an alien land
under the rule of a pale, slight and ghostly
                        and alien man?

you laugh
you drink
and for a moment
your pain is gone.
but i am here to tell you:
it is not over.
a thousand thousand betrayals hound you
among even those of you
dancing on this very water.
it is not over.
he is only dead.
he is not yet through
with you.

The Head of Luís Congo Cries Out for Water

agua
agua
agua—
if there is among you any congo man
any man with but a grain of pity in his soul
give me a drink of water as i die.
but look
look they cry out in their festive voices
the head of luís congo
it speaks
it begs a drop of water
the head of the great murderer
our torturer
the head of luís congo cries out for water

The Head of Luís Congo Weeps

olurun bon dié mystère
here am i at the crossroads of death and life
i look out across a standing water
to the land of the dead—mpemba—
where i can not enter whole
and weep:
o mbanza kongo
where are you now?
i look and look
but i do not see
o mbanza kongo
i search but i can not find out
the streets of my ancestors
nor any relative to receive me
o holy mountain
high ground of my striving
source of every drop of blood upon my severed hands
what is to become of me

wasting in some petit farmer's field
severed
rotting
burnt almost to ash
o sacred mountain
is this the doing of my two hands
and where are they now
olurun   bon dié   mystère
how am i fallen
now that my head is mounted on high?

The Head of Luís Congo Calls for His Medicine

o great god   good god
where is my healing powder
the balm to soothe to cleanse anoint and calm
my head
my heart
my two strong severed hands
crushed beyond recognition
and burnt to solid ash?
bon dié   olurun
do not let the dogs
the crow, the beasts of the field
do not let them feed upon me.
mystère   mystère
where now is my little pouch
my paquet d'medecin
my healing bag?
where now are my banganga des mystères
who cleaned my head and heart and hands
and told such great things for my life?
where is my little bag
my faith
my medicine from this evil day?

The Head of Luís Congo Confesses His Sin

silence! all of you, silence!
i tell you i am the head of luís congo and i speak for him.
enough
enough
enough.
mbanza kongo rises in the distance now.
she rises but i cannot see her heights.
she rises but my ashen feet cannot find her golden paths.
she rises and i stand on high
blinded to the glory i have set before my ways.
enough then.
it is true.
i have killed.
i have captured.
i have tortured.
and when i could not kill or capture
i maimed as best i could.
at my hands
at my very words
men, women, children
the agèd and those with child
fell down in heaps along the waters of the bayou.
many a soul
from many a nation
did i send on the watery mpemba way.
my pockets my house even my bed
were lined with gold
white gold
yellow gold
the gold of earth's roses.
and with every golden death among you
my house of gold rose higher and higher
nearer and nearer
the land of the ancestors.

and i became
every day
closer to their way.
and all of you—
congo men and mongrel nations alike
all of you
lived with the very intimate fear
of my good killing hand.
it is all
all of it
most certainly true.

The Head of Luís Congo Has His Little Say

congo tiamca matinga
colango bambara senegal
negro creole and more—
it is a good thing to live in fear of a mighty man.
it is a good thing to cross the water of death
being sacrificed on the altars of the king.
i came as you came
a minor man
crossing not one but two deathly waters.
and with every one of your heads
the gold in the seams of my pants
the gold in the posts of my house
the gold in the four corners of my field
the gold between the jambes of my mulata
the gold in the waters beside my great house grew
and grew
and paved the road—ever higher—to my greatness.
and what if i made myself a king?
this is a strange land.
a nether man's land.
and it is a good thing to be hated and feared—
is it not—
in a strange man's land.

it is true
it is true
it is true:
i captured and i killed and did not look back
and now i am captured and killed and cannot see farther.
but i did not take from you your healing medicines.
i did not take from you your human qualities.
i sent you—every one of you—
whole to the ancestors
and now you stand behind the walls of blessèd mbanza kongo
laughing in your teeth
cursing the demise
of a mighty man
who helped you from your lowly life bondage
along the great mpemba way.
a curse for the peace you have in that great city
and i languish.

The Head of Luís Congo Begs a Favor

i am the head of luís congo.
and i have one small request from him.
if you cannot bend to give me back my medicine bag
then burn it with my ashes.
if you cannot lift up my eyes from where they droop along my cheeks
if you cannot lift them
so that i can see the great god
so that i can see the great city i will never enter whole—
i tell you
i am the severed head of luís congo.
i speak for him—
in the name of the fear and hatred you once knew of me
give me please
i beg of you
a bit of your cool
       fair
       water.

Expeditus

"you say you believe
we are all the same in the end.
this is what you want to believe
now that you have your freedom.
let me tell you, wise man
i was born with this freedom and i do not trust the white man
       to pass me in the square without cutting me down.
       or his woman in her house there in the town
       to send him to cut me for a lark.
and i was born with the freedom
given you these last few days.
but because you are a christian
let me give you an example
so that you do not think hard of me.
here is an example.
you yourself are a christian.
you call yourself a christian and a catholic.
well so do i.
but with me it is a point of law.
freeborn as i am
i do not break the law when i can help it.
that as you can see is just good sense.
since i myself am a man of the law.
but let me show you.
st. expeditus.
you know the story.
they will not admit its truth
but everyone has heard the story by now.
a roman soldier.
a figure from a crowd,
a group scene intended for the foot of a crucifix.
a simple roman soldier.
not a warrior of distinction.
not a charioteer. no.
a foot soldier.

a member of a motley
and anonymous assembly.
and they lift him up.
they give him the status of sainthood.
and the laws on their books say we must carry out
   every crisis
   every moment of import in our lives
   under the offices of this holy catholic church.

"we are all the same you say.
and here they have us
   fools and cowards that we are, one,
   bending and praying
   to a painted plastered foot soldier.
we are all the same in the end, you say.
all the same.

"here is a figure i draw in the dirt.
a secular figure, clearly.
will you pray to it?
no. no. now you will not pray.
but you will go and kneel in the dust at the doors of their
  churches
and you will pray to a poor foot soldier
who never intended to be separated
from the rest of his kind.
you think your freedom buys you this.
and this
and this and this.
and i tell you i can not walk across that square
without knowing i can be cut down in a moment's passing.
or you—
your catechism
your rosary pressed to your bosom.
do you think this is why they got you your freedom
—the brothers of the lodge—
to make you free to kneel on dirt or stone floors at the backs

of churches
to see them swing the censers
to hear about the purgatory
set aside
for just such as your color and my own?
well.
enough of this.
here are papers to be made over.
what was your trade in bondage?
what did you do?"

"iron.
i worked in iron.
i helped to build the iron that holds the great houses secure.
i helped to build the gates the doors the windows and their
    bars.
throughout this whole city you can see my labor—
walls and gates and doors and windows
wrought of iron
and tempered all in vèvès.
i helped to make the curse
that cures this wretched city
that sends it year after year
into the great god's sea.

"you are freeborn, avocat.
        freeborn. and thus you think you must
        teach and reform a poor slave brother.
yes i stand and kneel outside their churches.
yes i cover my head in crosses and choke on dust.
i pray to expedite
because i know the labor of waiting
of biding time.
do i care if he is false or true?
do i care if he is given me in ignorance or else to throw me
    into confusion?
you say he is but a foot soldier.

well i have been a slave
a slave and a foot soldier too.
you think i have not been on forced marches to
        their spanish colonies to the east?
        or that i do not know that you too were made to go?
you think i have not served to guard this walled city
roused out of sleep or loving or dreaming i was loving
        there in the quarters behind the great house?
when you have been a slave
what is the indignity of a foot soldier?

"i tell you that i have prayed to expeditus.
        speed o speed o fast deliver me
        here are chains that bind me
        here are stones that weight me
        succor
        mercy
        and a quick deliverance
yes.
i have prayed these very words, avocat.
and i will live to see you pray them
as you cut across the square."

The Business of Pursuit: San Malo's Prayer

A Ritual Poem for J. B. Borders IV

1.

you walk the high road
between this land and the other
this dream and another
and are not free.
displacement
is a thing you know
at least as well
as your own good name.
a thing you have known
since setting foot on this man's shore
since taking your place
your woman
your house
on the high ground
on that man's high road.
or so you've been told.
       (and we've all been told
       —those of us young and sleek and determined enough
       not so very unlike you
       as the others would have us think)
so you have been told.
       (or thought
       or hoped
       or dreamt you knew all along)
your dreams run all the same these days.
in your vision
the heads are bloodless on their poles
mask-heads laid aside in their season—
eyeless, sightless, speechless things.
i stand outside your dreams
a hundred changeless years later.

i see your slightened and imperfect heart
—heart in a basket—
a bushel basket filled up with yams.
i see you braving the dark night of your dreams
and dutifully engaged
in the business of pursuit—
o great o great o great
deceiver.

i see you dream among the quiet known to be final.
i see your dream descend in calm when all is done.
i see your ungloved hands
and your eyes that look away in the opposite direction
—it does not matter—
i see you as if from so great a distance
i can not say
"he is coming
or going"—
i see only your form.
perhaps it is all i am able to see
—and so unlike any other form and perfect—
i lean forward in my desire, my prayer
until the roots fall from my head.
you are but gone.
i take my men, my women along the river road.
we go a-hacking and a-slashing
our bloody ungloved hands a-steaming—
we taste your freedom, luís congo.
your dying prayer,
your dying prayer,
brother.

2.

the night is a bastard gleaming
a leaning
a steaming

and full of questing.
at some point we all go questing in the night.
i say at one point it is all the same.
at some point the silence deepens.
the dark deepens
looses itself upon the city
—remorse
desire
regret
possibility—
the dark comes and shuts down upon us like a window
—the single
steaming
solitary
night—
i say it is then that we act.
i say i am afraid.
and i admit it.
i stand before you, beside you and afraid of my own truth, our
    truth.
afraid to lose the night loosing around, upon me
deepened
seamless
and silent
ici–dedans
com' peur
and cornered like a dog
in the heat of pursuit.

in this moment
i call my prayers about me and i act.

3.

the night is long.
the night is dark,
altogether seamless long and dark.
your eyes like mine make into gaping pools of unrest.

and yet you are brave. brave.
this is *our* darkness.
our night.
we have grown lean with much waiting.
we toss aside the makeshift covers like so many flags.
we bare our teeth and glisten—
our truest selves.
we pick up the bushel baskets of our hearts
a-slashing and a-hacking through the dark.

4.

big river
big muddy
big muddy shining water.
there are saints and spirits and loa without number.
i lean back on my heels looking out across the water.
i hold your traitor's heart inside my own, luís congo.
i do not see them coming
but i know that they are.
and this is how i know your hundred-year secret:
you must have had your vision
as i am having mine of you now
the emptied sockets
the eyelessness your own doing
blinded as you must have been, congo man
by the mulata, the first gold-piece they gave you,
the house standing up above the rest
on higher higher ground.
you pressed
your lips and teeth and tongue in the service of your white
     masters
—the lot of them
and only one of you—
a slave at heart for all your wealth, they say.
i say different.
i say the traitor's heart is long and wide and deep as any

other's.
what do you say, señor? m'sieu?
what could you say to those your brethren in the flesh?
could you say that you were special?
or saved?
could you say, "là, i see you in the sightless dark
coming with your evil down the white man's road"?
could you say you saw the river road, the men, the women
their elderly and children and those with child?
could you go before your own dressed in the white man's fine
         thin clothes
bearing your bloodshot eyes
your caul in your own bloodstained hands?
the road, broken, mending
and where it led to in the night?
o, i know you now m'sieu congo
brother, kindred
         mo vous connay bien fort
you are here among us now.
tonight, even as we pray and call and beckon.
among just so damned a crew as we you got your treatment
—revenge, respite, the holiest of reckonings—
         ici-present m'sieu congo, je vous sense
you speak the right languages.
you have your proper tongue, as we say in butcher-spanish,
but it is i, i
san malo, have your tongue.
i have your very own bushel basket.
and i say the dark is long and very very deep.
i do not see them coming but i know they come.
         o señor
         m'sieu
         je vous connais en fin
         et avec chacun des blancs je fais tué
         en fin je gout ta sangue nègre
         en fin mo mo trouve capab' di'
         c'est mo, congo

112

c'est mo vous voyé à la rue de la rive
congo congo
your hundred-year vision is true at last.
c'est mo
my head towering above the others
calling to you from atop this high ground:
o petit-coeur si nèg' et si souffrant
give the white man in all this tumult at least his due:
when the blacks fell upon you on that fated day
he did not even stop to tighten his little bag of coins.
does not the proverb say, my brother:
when you must kill the snake
cut out also his tongue?

and who knows
that in another hour and other skin than this
—blood of your same blood that i am—
i would not have done the same?
only i and the great god.
my head goes up on the pole just as you decreed.
even so, m'sieu congo
in spite of treacherous blood
bushel basket and the like
my tongue is mine
and black as night.

5.

i say it is all the same.
i say there are angels
black angels
congo angels
free black congo angels
all singing the same songs
one hundred, two hundred years.

how free can any of us have been?
how different is a traitor's heart than that of any slave?
and how free?
i say luís congo looked out from his highest tower
            and cursed the dark, the land, his own slave-heart.
i say he saw them with their heads jammed to their poles
            and spat into the wind and cursed the night.
i say it is no small thing to betray one's own.
i say he had a vision and a lust for life as deep as any slave's.
but i can see them
—angels—
            in the middle of the day
            along the river road even as we speak.
i call the names of my gods
            —damballah
            papa legba
            yemanjá
            ilê fa ne wô—
i say when the moment comes
and the eyes are fully open
it lasts for but a second and then we are done for.
i only know the histories, the myths
what others tell me
and what my gods say to be true.

one other small thing:
i have never been to the chapelroom at ms. timotea's.
but when i go
i set my light on the altar of san malo.

Suicide City

i turn in bed toward my lover
how his skin
hugs to the bony parts
nothing in excess
and nothing missing.
my lover's eyes are closed.
my lover's eyes are often closed.
he cannot see
the fine trophy i make of his fine hide
the smell of him clinging
and the forbidden thing
the forbidden thing between us like a weight.

night and day and night still following upon night
the coming of spring is a difficult thing.
we here in the city
mornings stand about a lumpen horde
all our smells commingled with the city air
with dust and traffic
cheap greasy breakfasts transported in bags by working-men—
faces altogether lacking in sleep—
smelling as they do of hard soap and unfinished coffees
school-children with their knapsacks loaded down with nothing
                    of value
we stand about the bus stops and press against each other
                    when it comes
we are grateful for a seat and turn our heads to windows or to
    books
to newspapers or one another
we are grateful to have such destinations
obligations that remove us
from ourselves
we nod and tip good-mornings
we hum inside the humming streetcar
we hum inside our humming bodies

and all our secrets safe at least for now.

night in the city is a maddening deafening
opening
of hot blossoms
azalea
jasmine
cereus
great roses brought by europeans long ago
sweet olive pouring over weekend stench
we pour ourselves into the city streets
or lock ourselves behind our doors
its doors
or else we turn and turn beneath plain sheets
and ceiling fans
our mouths our lovers' mouths
our hands their hands
we turn and turn
and do not look away

sex inside the city is almost communal.
the street creeps in
the children across the gate
the sirens and the shouts of drunks
the poor
the mad
the broken
the late
we cry out together
in time to hear their cries.
we look ahead to sweat and moans to come
collapse and seize ourselves each other
we do not whisper
cause we know no one cares:
their lovers all are boarding streetcars at the track.

long long long the night it has no end.

we moan and turn and call on names we had forgotten.
we pull ourselves up by our feet.
we drink night–water
taste our mouths that taste of spit and kisses
urinate longer than we care to
scratch our behinds
look out windows
meander back to bed
we sleep there.
or hump.
or say "are you alright" for absolutely no reason.
we do not listen to the outside.
we know that it lurks.
it listens.
it knows our names.

the forbidden thing between us like a weight
it waits until we sleep
and then
the city all around us and we dream
all together in our tribe we dream the city back to sleep
we shield our fears
lovers
turning
ever turning in the night
the city dreams us back alive
and all our dreams forbidden
thrumming
eternal
at the track.

meditation is an urban preoccupation.
country people poke fun, they laugh.
here in the city
we all go mad together and simply refuse to tell.
we are so superior
we meditate

we spout the latest world report
we lock church doors
pay tax on candles and prayer cards
sing under our breaths walking the bright streets at night
we practice breathing last breaths
—but we have not forgotten how to sing—
we open our mouths and are wise
nights we go home to one another
fearful of the sounds
the smells of spring
a difficult thing to deny
our confidence
a thing left at the door
a useful thing sure
but home is home after all
and there we are alone and naked for all the city to see.
hurry
hurry we want to warn one another
it comes
it dreams
it knows our names.

the city looked up one day and was free.
not from yellow fever or flood or torrents of affliction
not whoring or debt or the stench of standing waters
not from cults of destitution
the union roosting, its naive bravado
coteries of saviors bearing bibles in arms:
all in that way abiding.
it happened that way didn't it?
was that the way it was?
whole city of slaves
name of jude eulalie andré amalie josefina adelína ambrose martinet
ariane flavio zuma placide adão obade mattoso teresinha jérémie
mathieu hilaire robért roseangela marcus albertine nicolette cúde
jean-lùc louis luís théard théophile ti-nom ti-bert ti-jean ti-ton
down from kongo senegambe são tomé nzadi ngola san domingue

118

over waters of the dead:
large river river nzadi river kongo
river atlantic
to mesachabe
big-muddy-big-water all over again.
and so the city looked up that one day and was free
free from the indigo the brick factory
the cane fields the rice fields
but oh the bordellos the church the households
the ward heelers the back rooms the dirty linen
the cigar factories the baker shops
the little merchants and their small merchandise
cigar-rollers shoemakers praline-women sawyers wainwrights
the lavatrice the coachman the drayman the cook
the builder
the builder
but oh the city looks back and says its own name and who answers?
who hears?
not drums alone
but also the bare foot against red brick
against italian marble sometimes or tile
the blue-brown-violet throats of bad or good children
of old men keening
harpish voices of women too young to be so old
the closing of a rheumy cataracted eye
the swallow of bloodied throat late into the knife-fight no one
    wins
the evergoing thrumming of the night
the hard summer days
the sounds of leaves about to fall
sound of a papa's voice from his tomb
the doors that scrape and close and hesitate to scrape and close
sound of that river turning on its belly our belly
the near-words of the near-dead

again

in this city
in *this* city
everything comes again
where we take nothing to the streets
it waits for us there and is it any wonder
is it any wonder
we wander through the slick the dark the foul-sweet streets
in all this darkest black of night
where some round-headed boy
centuries younger than he knows
claps hands to keyboard or to horn
to microphone or congo-cheek
and says so softly
someone gave this song to me?

every night
every single night
it happens in exactly this way
inside this city
that someone's child should say that thing
that we would go to hear and see him say it
would tell him
play oh play that thing
that horn that key that drum that throat that thing you play
*just **play** it baby*
and all our secrets safe
at least for now?

we go home.
we go home turn keys in doors and laugh and do not forget.
in this city nothing has been forgotten.
that one great sin we cannot claim.
it knows
it waits
it comes again
we see it in the eyes we come on in the street
we see it in the eyes of lovers turning away or toward us
we see it in the braces of the streetcar tracks

we hear it taste it feel it breathe it in each day
every day
we are so wise
we go home
we are so hip
we go home
we are so faithful in our turning
it comes on us unawares
and then we sweat.

oh but the city is not fooled.
it knows it is the lover who is not blind but merely sleeps.
it knows we know it is the dreamer
turning huge back
away from us to hump
toward us to dream
to dream us back alive each night
so that we wake
thrumming
eternal
ever
at the tracks.

GLOSSARY OF NEW ORLEANS
ETHNIC EXPRESSIONS,
PLACE NAMES, AND CHARACTERS

aguardiente [Spanish/Portuguese: *agua* + *ardiente*, literally, "burning water"] cane liquor; a coarse, rumlike alcoholic beverage distilled from sugarcane, manufactured and drunk by the slaves of Louisiana, the Caribbean, Latin America; used also as spiritual offering or libation.

alligator-pear the avocado

avocat [French] lawyer.

back-a-town [literally, "in back of the town"] indicating direction or location behind or below a given street or section of town; also, any area thus designated; because New Orleans follows the crescent of the Mississippi River, there is no true north, south, east, west; directions thus refer to landmarks, areas, bodies of water: *e.g.*, back-a-town, front-a-town, lake-side, riverside.

bamboula a ring dance of African origin danced by slaves and free Blacks in eighteenth- and nineteenth-century New Orleans.

Banganga des Mystères [Ki-Kongo, pl. of *nganga*, ritual expert + Haitian Creole *Mystère*, spirit, deity] loosely, priests, priestesses, diviners; the Banganga heal with roots, herbs, and charms and venerate the most ancient and highest ranking among the dead.

banqette a paved or boarded sidewalk

Bayou Road the road running parallel to and following the curve of Bayou St. John in New Orleans; formerly known also as the High Road.

Bayou St. John a bayou is any marshy inlet or outlet of a lake or other body of water; Bayou St. John, located in downtown New Orleans, has served for Black New Orleanians since the 1700s as a meeting place for religious and other rituals and festivals.

Bon Dié [Creole< French *Bon Dieu*, literally, *Good God*] the Great God of the African slaves of New Orleans; not necessarily identical to the Christian god, Bon Dié is all-knowing, all-powerful.

butcher-spanish the now defunct creolized Spanish of Louisiana, imported via Cuba during the Spanish colonial period (broadly, 1763–1803).

Canal (Street) the broad street forming the dividing line between downtown and uptown New Orleans, formerly and respectively, the French/Creole and American "cities" comprising New Orleans.

chamy bag [Creole, *chamois* (fabric)] a small or large pouch, usually with a drawstring, containing one's personal medicine or juju; originally made of chamois fabric

chapelroom that room, in the homes of Hoodoos, and often their devotees, used for religious and spiritual practice, consultation, meditation, etc.

Congo, Tiamca, Matinga, Colango, Bambara, Nago, Senegal, Creole, Negro designations of Africans transported as slaves to Louisiana during the Spanish colonial period. The word *Creole* was applied to enslaved Africans born in the New World; also, to the language spoken by them and their descendants.

Congo, Luís a free Kongo man who in 1726 was employed in New Orleans as keeper of the High or Bayou Road, where he established a plantation estate; the official executioner of slaves escaping New Orleans via Bayou St. John, he is said to have died mysteriously at the hands of slaves.

conju [conjure] the practice of conjuring or other spiritual trade and practice associated with **Hoodoo.**

Damballah [Fon, *Dan* or *Dan Bada;* also Kongo, *Da* or *Dan;* also Kongo, *Ndamba,* literally, "rainbow serpent"] that deity who mediates between the worlds of the living and dead.

doc/doctor in New Orleans Hoodoo, one who employs roots, herbs, ritual, etc., to heal body and mind, thus often referred to as a "two-headed doctor."

Érzulie Haitian representation of Yoruba deity Ochun or Oshun, goddess of the river waters.

ex voto [Latin, literally, "from a vow"] a votive offering, such as a picture, medal, or other small emblem left in a shrine or other holy place as a symbol of devotion or thanksgiving.

faubourg [French, literally, "false town, false borough"] any of the early, named suburbs and districts of New Orleans, such as the Faubourg Marigny or the Faubourg Tremé (see **Tremé, Faubourg**).

fix Hoodoo terminology for "spell" or "bad medicine"; used as both noun and verb: *to fix* or *put a fix on* someone, something, or a situation.

Hoodoo in New Orleans and much of southeast Louisiana, a religious and spiritual belief system governing and encompassing all life and life principles including, but not limited to, rituals, mysteries, healing, protection from evil, conjuring, interpretation of dreams and signs, as well as proper care of the dead and ritual veneration of the ancestors; the fundamental practices and principles of Hoodoo are West African and Caribbean in origin; it is related to but not synonymous with *Vodùn, Obeah, Macumba, Candomblé, Santería, Santidade,* and other New World African religions.

loa [Yoruba] spirit, deity.

lower nine reference to the Ninth Ward, one of seventeen wards or civil districts in New Orleans.

m'dear [Creole< *mother dear*] mama, maman; an endearment often conferred on older women without regard for family status.

Mbanza Kongo [Ki-Kongo] in Kongo cosmology, the ideal capital to which the holy departed return, situated on a hilltop and ruled by a mighty and beloved king; also, the ancient capital of the Kongo kingdom, renamed São Salvador under Portuguese colonial rule in the mid-sixteenth century.

misbelieve New Orleans name for the Japanese plum tree common throughout the area; a mild table wine, sometimes used as a curative, is made from the bright orange fruit.

mòn [Creole< French *maman*] mother; familiar or contemptuous usage, depending on the context.

Mother any woman who serves as a healer, especially one who operates a private chapel or has a sizable following.

Mother Catherine healer and saint of the Spiritual church of New Orleans.

Mpemba [Ki-Kongo, literally, *chalk, white substance* (the color white representing death, the dead, mourning)] Kongo Land of the Dead, represented as a vast body of water; in Kongo cosmology, the earth is a mountain situated above Mpemba.

Mystère [Haitian Creole, literally, "(the) Mystery"] Great God Almighty.

Papa Legba [Creole< Yoruba *Elegba, Elegbara, Elegua*] representation of Yoruba deity *Elegba* or *Elegua,* guardian of the sacred doorway, the crossroads, and emissary of the gods; he is justice personified.

paquet d'medecin [Creole, literally, "medicine bag"] a small or large pouch or other bag containing one's personal medicine, made up of various sacred objects; **chamy bag.**

pòn [Creole< French *papa*] father; familiar or contemptuous usage, depending on the context.

prayer band term applied to any "renegade" (usually Christian) religious group organized by women.

Rampart (Street) the broad street running north–south and separating the Vieux Carré (French Quarter) from the Faubourg Tremé

St. Expedite/Expeditus [pronounced "ex-pe-*deet*"] grantor of speedy response; a "false" saint of the Catholic church; according to legend, a statue of a foot soldier intended for a crucifixion scene arrived separately from the other figures and the word "Expedite" was mistaken for his name.

St. Martin de Porres [d. 1639, Peru] Black saint of Lima and patron of the poor, de Porres was a member of the Dominican order; son of an African mother, whose name has apparently been "lost," and Don Juan de Porres.

San Malo, Juan rebel leader of a maroon colony at Chef Menteur, on the eastern outskirts of New Orleans; when captured, San Malo and his followers were hanged. A major figure in New Orleans and regional folk history, he is remembered as a martyr in such songs and ballads as "Aye! Zheun Gens." In "The Business of Pursuit: San Malo's Prayer," I have invented a mythical relationship between San Malo and **Luís Congo.**

Seven Sisters a family of holy women said to have lived in and around New Orleans at the turn of the twentieth century.

shallow water loa-mama a traditional chant invoking the blessings of Spirit of the Waters.

slave-bricked descriptive of any road, street, building or other structure constructed all or in part of the common red brick found throughout New Orleans and originally manufactured by the slaves of the city's first brick factory, located in the Faubourg Tremé; the handiwork of slave ancestors, the bricks are believed to possess spiritual power and are used most frequently to bless and purify the homes of the faithful by rubbing across steps and doorways; used also for drawing vèvès on stone, wood, paper, etc.

Sor Juana the sister of St. Martin de Porres, of whom nothing is known.

sortilège [French, literally, "sorcery, magic"] in traditional Hoodoo, the ritual of tying of knots, symbolizing the binding or sealing of a situation or condition.

Spanish Fort site of Spanish colonial fort on Bayou St. John at the northwest outlet to Lake Pontchartrain; now part of City Park in the area bounded by Robert E. Lee, Ibis, and Beauregard Streets.

Tremé, Faubourg the first suburb of the original city of New Orleans (Vieux Carré); settled in the 1710s by free Blacks, and now part of down-town New Orleans.

vèvè the sign, symbol, or signature of a deity in the form of a diagram, series of ideographs, or other visual representation.

BIOGRAPHY

BRENDA MARIE OSBEY received the B.A. from Dillard University, the M.A. from the University of Kentucky, and also attended the Université Paul Valéry at Montpéllier, France.

She is the author of *Desperate Circumstance, Dangerous Woman* (Story Line Press, 1991), *In These Houses* (Wesleyan University Press, 1988), and *Ceremony for Minneconjoux* (Callaloo Poetry Series, 1983; University Press of Virginia, 1985). Her poems have appeared in numerous journals, anthologies, and collections, including *Callaloo; Obsidian; Essence; Southern Exposure; Southern Review; Early Ripening: American Women's Poetry Now; The Made Thing: An Anthology of Contemporary Southern Poetry; 2PLUS2: A Collection of International Writing; Epoch; American Voice;* and *American Poetry Review.*

In 1993 she received a Louisiana Division of the Arts Fellowship and a New Orleans Jazz and Heritage Foundation Maxi-Grant. She is the recipient also of the National Endowment for the Arts Creative Writing Fellowship in 1990, a 1984 AWP (Associated Writing Programs) Poetry Award, and the Academy of American Poets Loring-Williams Award in 1980. She has been a fellow of the MacDowell Colony, the Fine Arts Work Center in Provincetown, the Kentucky Foundation for Women, the Virginia Center for the Creative Arts, the Millay Colony, and the Bunting Institute of Radcliffe College, Harvard University.

She has taught French and English at Dillard University in New Orleans, African American and Third World literatures at the University of California at Los Angeles, African American literature and creative writing at Loyola University, and was visiting writer-in-residence at Tulane University.

Brenda Marie Osbey is a native of New Orleans.

Printed in the United States
33507LVS00017B/16-54

9 780807 121986